CW01402482

 SCIENCE IN OUR WORLD

MATERIALS

Contributory Author
Brian Knapp, BSc, PhD
Art Director
Duncan McCrae, BSc
Science advisor
Jack Brettle, BSc, PhD,
Chief Research Scientist, Pilkington plc
Special scientific models
Tim Fulford, MA, Head of Design and Technology,
Leighton Park School
Editorial consultant
Rita Owen, BSc
Special photography
Ian Gledhill
Print consultants
Landmark Production Consultants Ltd
Printed and bound in Hong Kong
Produced by
EARTHSCAPE EDITIONS

First published in the United Kingdom in 1993
by Atlantic Europe Publishing Company Limited,
86 Peppard Road, Sonning Common, Reading,
Berkshire, RG4 9RP, UK

Publication Data
Knapp, Brian
   Materials – (Science in our world; 28)
   1. Materials – For children
   I. Title II. Series
620.11

      ISBN 1-869860-18-7

In this book you will find some words that have been shown in **bold** type. There is a full explanation of each of these words on pages 46 and 47.

Experiments that you might like to try for yourself have been put in a yellow box like this.

Acknowledgements
The publishers would like to thank the following:
Irene Knapp, Leighton Park School, Dr Angus McCrae,
Redlands County Primary School, Elaine Rimmer,
Sonning Common Garages and Marcia Young.

Picture credits
t=top b=bottom l=left r=right
All photographs are from the Earthscape Editions library
except the following: Tim Fulford 31t, 31b.

Contents

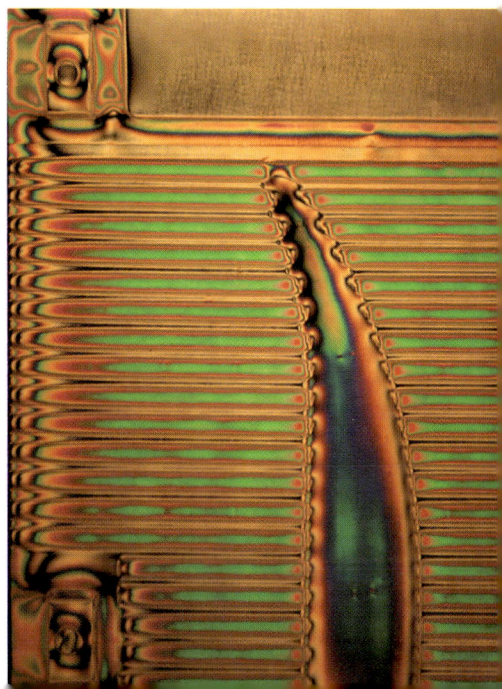

Introduction

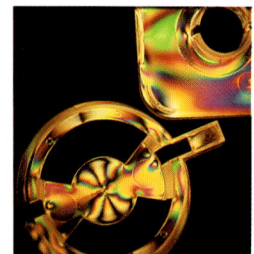
Matter is the general word for all materials. Materials are types of matter with recognisable names such as water, lead and cotton.

Some materials are made of single substances. Diamonds, for example, contain nothing but the single **element** called carbon. But most things are more complicated than this. The pages of this book, for example, are made of a material called paper. Paper is a **manufactured** material which is made from even more basic, or **raw materials**, tree trunk **fibres** and quarried clay.

Tree fibre that makes the bulk of paper is an **organic material**, that is it has been made by living things. Coal, wood, cork, oil and skin are all organic materials. Of the eleven billion substances known in the world, ten billion of them contain carbon and are produced from organic raw materials.

The clay that gives the paper its smooth feel is a rock, and it is an **inorganic material**. Sand and lava, limestone and granite are all examples of inorganic materials.

Of the enormous variety of materials to choose from, some, such as cork, occur naturally (they are **natural materials**), while others, such as plastics, have been made by scientists (called **synthetic materials**).

Each material has its own range of properties, which makes it more suitable for some uses than others. If materials with the wrong properties are chosen, the results can be very obvious. What would you think, for example, if a fizzy-drink maker used bottles which leaked gas and left the drink 'flat'?

Using unsuitable materials can also lead to tragedy. For example some unsuitable home furnishings have too easily caught fire.

Start to find out about materials in any way you choose. Just turn to a page to begin your discoveries.

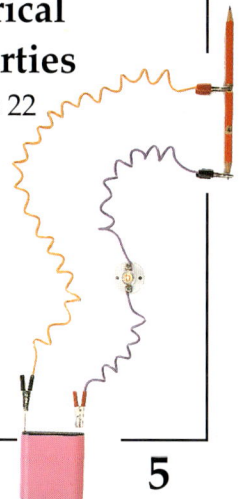

Natural materials

Natural materials are all around us. They can be used, for example, to make the walls of our homes, the furniture we use and the clothes we wear.

Nature also provides us with the raw materials that can be modified to produce other materials such as some metals or even synthetic materials such as plastics.

However, there are many things in nature that we cannot yet copy. For example, the **adhesive** that holds a barnacle to a rock or the flexibility of **cells** that let a flower stem bend with the wind.

Adhesives and shock-resistant materials

Barnacles and mussels are unable to move by themselves to catch food so instead they attach themselves to rocks where the tide rises and falls. These can be places where waves break fiercely during storms. These tiny creatures can cling to slippery rocks and withstand the crashing of waves far better than a sea wall.

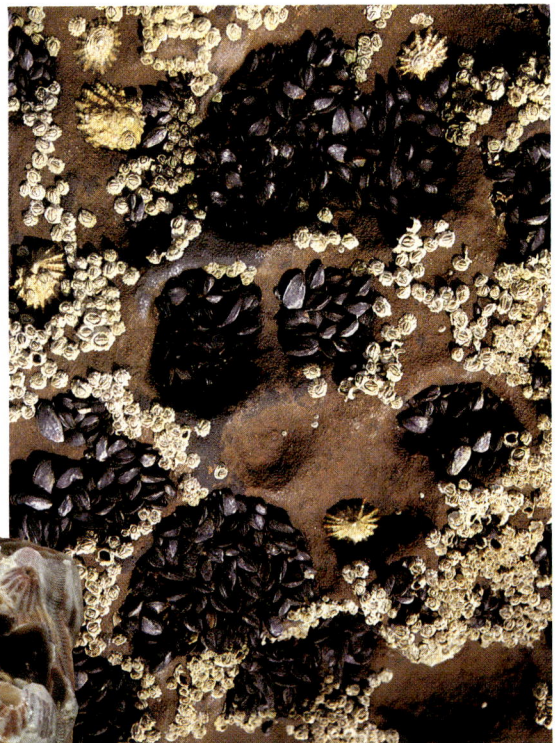

The shells of barnacles are made up of plates of calcium carbonate that can stand up to the shock of battering waves. Part of the **strength** is in the material, part is in the domed shapes.

The natural adhesive that holds a barnacle to a rock will hold in wet and dry conditions. As yet there is no artificial glue that can do such a good job.

Fingernails are made of a substance called keratin.

Skin

Skin cells bind together to make sheets. As the top layer of skin is worn away new cells grow from the layers below to replace them. Skin is flexible, it will stretch and go back into shape, it will grip even in the wet. No artificial material has so many useful properties.

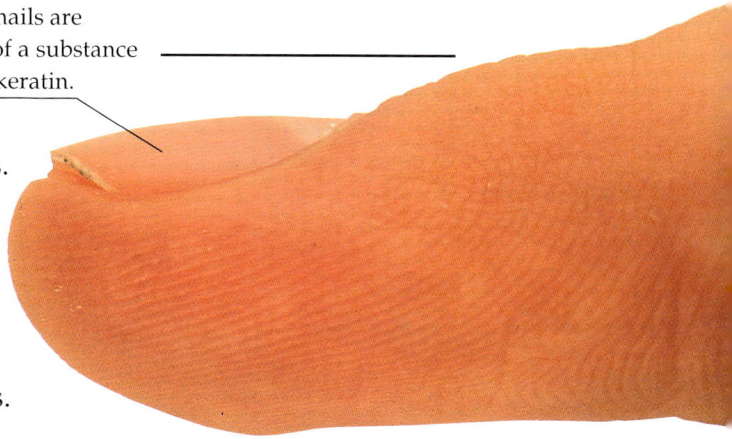

Shell

Some shells, such as seashells, are made up of chalky materials that not only give exciting colours, but allow the shell to be thin, lightweight and yet tough.

(For more information on how shape makes materials stronger see the book Shapes and structures *in the Science in our world series.)*

Flexible fibres

Many plants will yield fibres. The fan on the right, for example, is made from palm leaves (shown in the picture on the left).

Fibres are tough yet flexible and can be used for a variety of things including paper, **pulp** and cloth known as viscose.

Sap

The sap in some plants (such as the sugar cane) has a high sugar content and is used to produce natural sugar. Natural rubber, collected from tropical rubber trees, is another valuable sap. Some trees also exude resin from their bark. This has been widely used as a varnish for furniture.

Rubber, a natural sap from the rubber tree.

Raw materials

People have found many ways of processing naturally occurring materials to make an even wider range of materials with useful properties. In many cases, therefore, they are the raw materials for manufactured products. Here are some examples.

Plant and animal remains
Organic materials include wood, plant stems, dung, coal, oil and natural gas (Note: they can be used as fuels as well as raw materials).

Many organic materials are made from long strings of molecules or **polymers** which can be rearranged into synthetic materials such as **plastics**.

Metals
A rock containing useful amounts of metal is called an ore.

To extract the metal from the ore it has to be heated in special furnaces so that the metal can be separated from the rock.

Copper ore

Refined to make

Copper

Oil

Processed to make

Plastics (polymers)

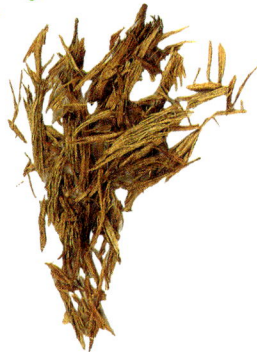

Wood fibre

Pulped to make

Paper

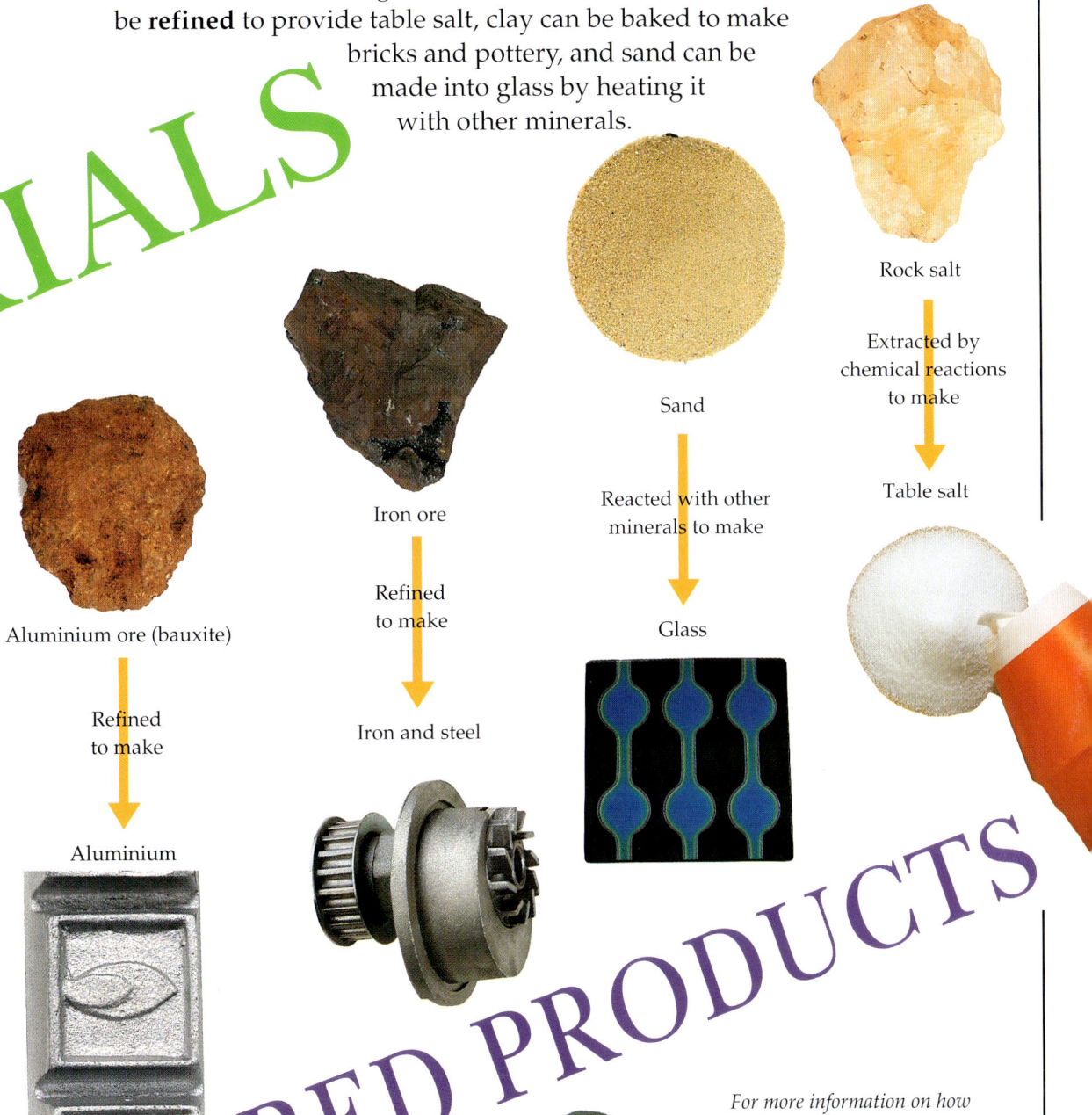

Minerals

Rocks are made of **minerals**. These can often be separated out and used to manufacture new materials. For example, the calcium carbonate in limestone can be used for making cement and fertilizer. Rock salt can be **refined** to provide table salt, clay can be baked to make bricks and pottery, and sand can be made into glass by heating it with other minerals.

Rock salt

Extracted by chemical reactions to make

Sand

Iron ore

Aluminium ore (bauxite)

Reacted with other minerals to make

Table salt

Refined to make

Refined to make

Glass

Aluminium

Iron and steel

For more information on how metals, minerals and organic materials are formed and where they are found on the Earth see the book How the Earth works *in the Science in our world series.)*

9

Choosing the best materials

When you look at many quite ordinary objects, such as toys or the appliances used in a kitchen, you may discover that each has been made from several different kinds of materials.

The choice of materials used has not been made by chance – the designers have selected each one because of its useful properties. For example, a material may have the strength needed, or be flexible, or have a smooth surface.

Aluminium conductor

Plastic insulation

Plastic cover to hold conductors in place.

Electrical cables

Cables bring electric power to our homes. There are millions of kilometres of cable in the world today, so each one needs to be cheap and easy to make. It must be able to **conduct** electricity efficiently, it must not 'leak' electricity to the ground (or cause danger to people) and it must be flexible so that it can be taken into awkward places.

Copper or aluminium are chosen for the cores of the cable because they conduct electricity well. Each conductor is surrounded with plastic which is both waterproof and an insulator. Buried cables are further protected from accidental damage by an aluminium or copper sheath. Aluminium and copper are commonly used because they do not readily **corrode**.

The copper wire sheath protects the conductor from accidental damage by digging machines when it is buried in the ground.

Plastic cover to keep the whole cable watertight.

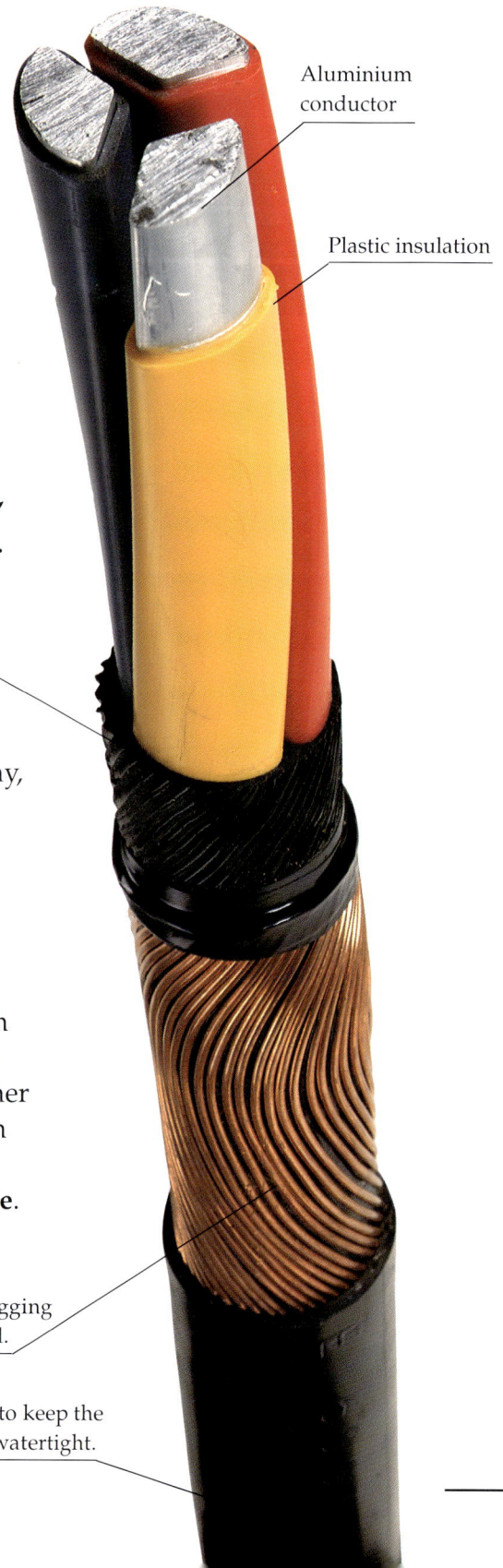

Snap connectors used to fit pieces together during assembly rely on the slightly springy property of some plastics.

Toys can be made more cheaply if large parts can be moulded as single items. Plastics are very suitable for precision mouldings of this kind.

Plastics will not readily accept paints, but the colour can be added to the plastic before it is moulded. This will give it scratch-resistant properties.

Toys

Toys are often like miniature versions of the real item. But because everything is small, the same materials cannot always be used on a miniature that were used on the original. For example, a full-sized wheel is made with steel, but a toy will be made by forcing liquid zinc or plastic into a mould and letting it set; lightweight bodies are made by forcing plastic into a mould.

Remarkable plastic bottles

Plastic bottles have to do many more jobs than one might at first think. Bottles for a fizzy drink need to withstand knocks and therefore have to be tough and not break. The material must be watertight and also gas tight so the fizz does not leak out, and it must be relatively stiff so the bottle holds its shape. It also must be capable of being moulded.

The bottles often need to be transparent, light weight and cheap, and if possible recyclable.

Polyethylene terephthalate (PET) is used for fizzy drink bottles because the cheaper polyvinyl chloride PVC is not as gas-tight and so it can only be used for still (unfizzy) drinks.

PET

PVC

The changing uses of materials

For many thousands of years people made use of natural materials simply by using their natural properties. But scientists have now developed many materials that allow manufacturers to build stronger, lighter and more versatile products.

During the **industrial revolution** items were **mass-produced** for the first time and many new products became available for the home. Of course, manufacturers still had to make their designs appropriate to the available materials. So, as soon as new materials such as plastics were developed, new designs could be developed as well.

Investigate change
In the nineteenth century iron and steel were used for many domestic articles such as the tin-plated baths shown in the picture below.

However, as soon as new materials were invented, designers seized on the opportunities to make items which were more comfortable and better suited to people's needs. Find out what materials are now used for making baths and the advantages of the new materials.

The use of unmodified raw materials limits what can be made. This traditional hut made by North American Indians of the Appalachian forests uses pieces of tree bark fixed over a frame of sticks. As elsewhere, such huts were quickly abandoned as the Indians developed more sophisticated techniques of house-making.

The natural properties of strength, pliability and insulation are better used when the tree is sawn into planks rather than left as timbers, as shown in this traditional New England church in the USA.

Modern large roofs are held up with steel because bigger unsupported spans can be achieved.

Old stone forts and castles are attractive to look at but they were difficult to build and not as strong as they appear.

Changes in buildings

Buildings show clearly the way changes followed the availability of improved materials. The properties of stone, for example, dictated the shape of the largest buildings. Today far bigger, stronger and lighter buildings can be constructed using steel frames and reinforced concrete.

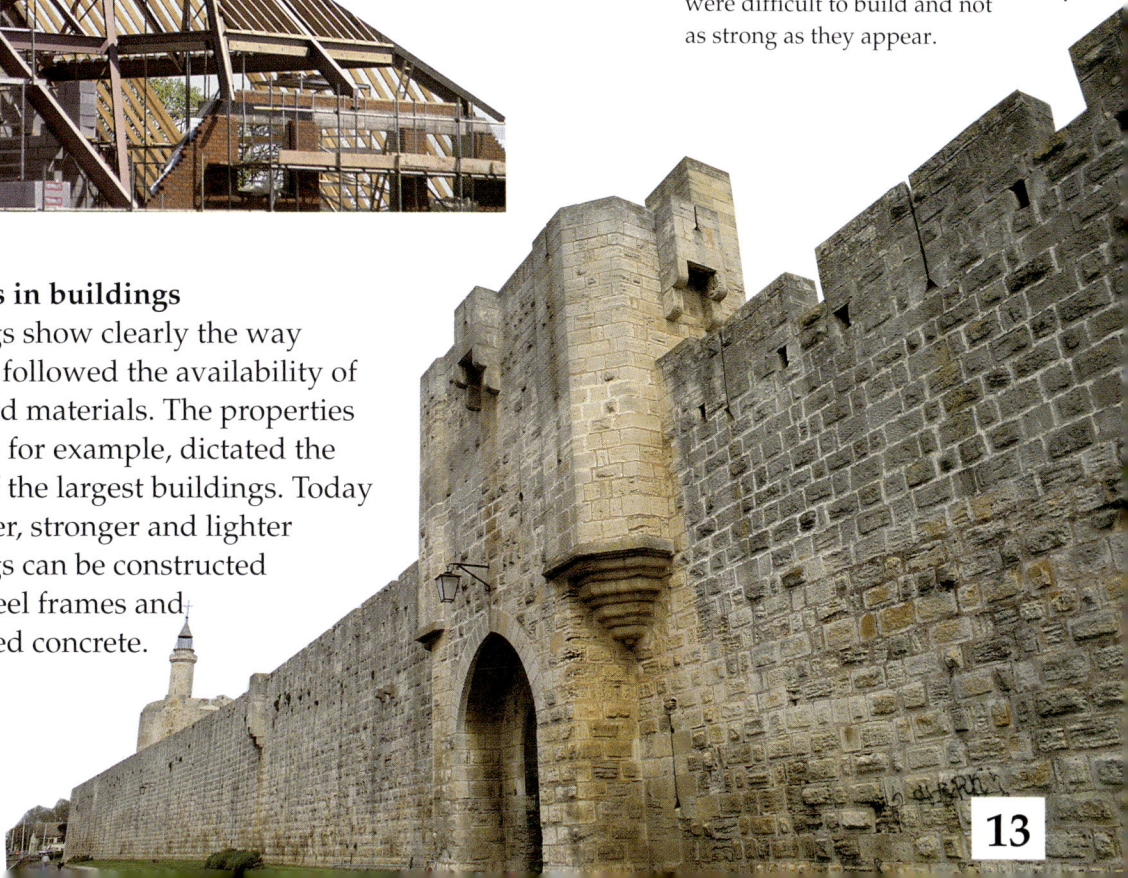

13

The effects of force

Scientists spend much of their time investigating the properties of materials in order to find out how they behave in a variety of situations. One of the most important properties is how a material responds to forces such as stretching and impact.

Force
When a material is pushed or pulled it may change shape (that is it **deforms**). However, the way it changes shape, whether it returns to its original shape, goes into a new shape or breaks apart varies with the force that is applied.

A rubber band being stretched elastically.

1 Elastic change
When enough force is applied to an object it deforms. However, when the force is removed the material will often return to its original shape. This is called an **elastic** change. A rubber band is good example of an elastic material.

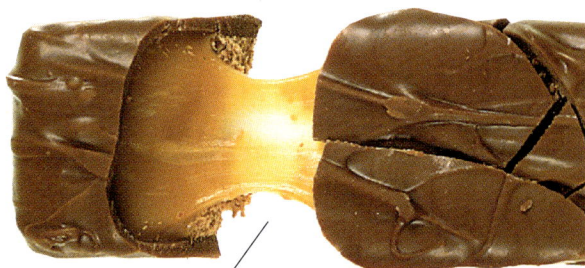

A snack bar at its plastic stage

2 Plastic change
When a larger force is applied a material may continue to deform, but if the force is now removed it will stay in this new shape. This is called a **plastic** change. Pulling a snack bar apart and bending a steel staple are examples of plastic change.

This twig has been bent beyond its plastic stage and it has fractured.

3 Break
If enough force is applied to a material it will become **brittle** and eventually break, or fracture.

(Be careful not to confuse the word plastic with the materials popularly called plastics which should correctly be called polymers. See page 26.)

The wire used for a paper staple has to be strong enough to hold papers together. If you try to prise it with your finger it will not yield.

The wire in a staple is chosen so that it will bend (become plastic) under the force from the stapler. Then, when it has bent, it must remain springy (elastic) to hold the paper firmly together.

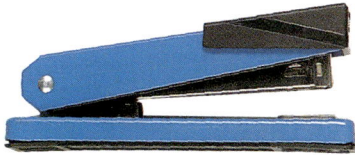

Steel is plastic when heated or when put under very high pressure. This enables ingots to be shaped into

Investigate the plastic properties of food
People rely on the plastic properties of pasta when they are rolling it out or when making spaghetti.

Feed a sheet of pasta through a pasta machine by turning the handle slowly. Look to see the way the pasta emerges from the machine. (This is called extrusion, see also page 33.)

Now feed another sheet through the machine, this time turning as fast as you can. Does the pasta still form into good rods or has the plastic limit been exceeded and is the result less satisfactory?

From your investigations, try to find out if there a best speed for deforming pasta.

A pasta machine producing 'rods' of spaghetti.

Investigate force

Every material has its special ways of behaving when a force is applied. Solids are usually at first springy (elastic), then pliable (plastic) and then they become brittle and break.

By contrast, some liquids become more and more stiff when they are stirred until they finally become solids.

Liquids to solids

The white of an egg is a liquid. If you pour it from one container to another it instantly moulds itself to the shape of the new container.

Liquids flow because the molecules of the egg white are not fixed rigidly together. However, when an egg white is beaten dramatic changes occur. The transparent liquid becomes a white solid. In this case the fast whipping action makes the egg material into a foam of air bubbles and white.

Critical force

Find out about the forces needed to change a liquid into a solid by beating a mixture of cornflour and water using an electric mixer.

Begin by setting the mixer at a low speed (or 'blend'). Add water until the mixture is like cream.

Increase the speed and see if any changes occur. You should find that, at a certain speed of whisking (and therefore force from the beaters) the properties of the cornflour mix change and it behaves like a solid.

High speed
(whisk speed) for
a little longer.

Low speed
(blend speed)

Egg beater

High speed (whisk speed)
for a few minutes.

Egg white

1 The equipment

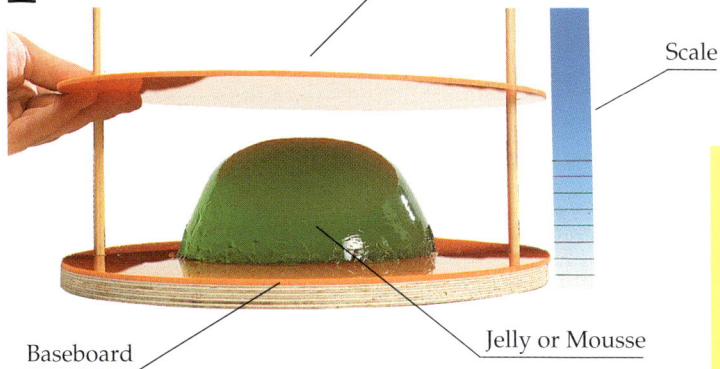

Top board slotted into supports to keep it horizontal.

Scale

Baseboard

Jelly or Mousse

2 Jelly at its elastic stage

Weight

The effects of pressure

Place a jelly between the boards and add weights. After adding each new weight take a scale reading and then take all the weights off and read the scale again. The first changes should be elastic and the jelly should return to its original height. A point will be reached when the jelly becomes plastic and will not return to its original shape. Finally the jelly will fracture into a frightful mess!

Try the experiment with other materials, such as mouse and bread (without the crust).

3 Jelly at its fracture stage

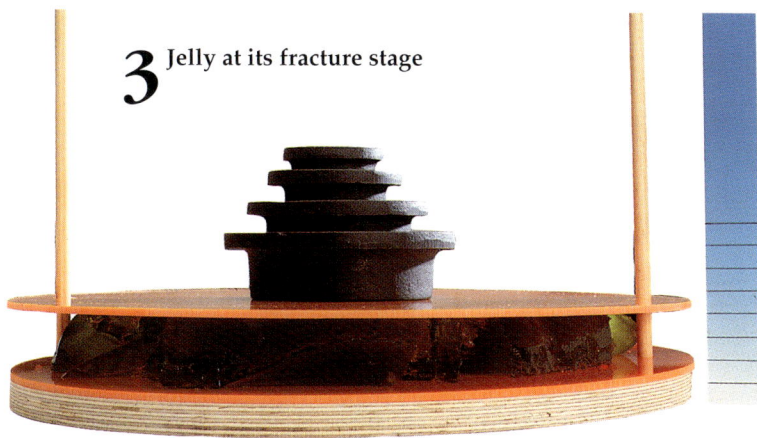

4 Failed jelly!

Finding hidden forces

Materials are often pushed through a die or squeezed into a mould. They are put under great pressure during the process and they 'remember' the **stresses**. Here is a way to investigate the hidden stresses in some plastics.

Stress in materials
Materials are put under enormous pressures when they are formed. Although under normal circumstances we cannot see this, such pressures remain as invisible 'scars' in the material. These are called stress lines.

Concentrations of stress lines show regions of weakness. It is important to be able to see the stress lines so that new designs can be made that remove any problem regions.

Stresses show up under a special light called polarized light as these pictures demonstrate.

Polarizing filter from a camera shop (or polarizing sunglass lenses).

This is the plastic front to a torch under investigation. The stress lines show that it was injection moulded from this point near one edge of the disk.

The plastic holders used to keep cans of drink together on the shop shelves show the stress lines clearly under polarizing filters.

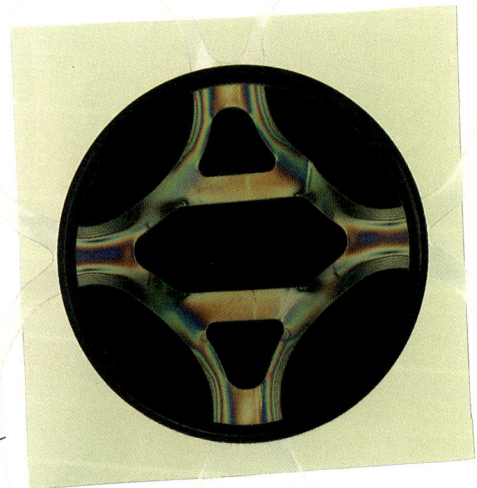

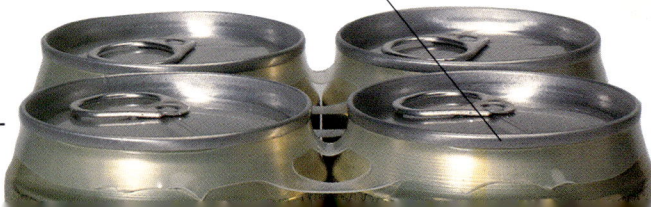

This stand to a shop-displayed product shows beautifully the stress marks involved during manufacture.

This are two sandwich bags. The top one has been stretched and the other has had a thumb pushed into it.

Hunt the hidden patterns
Find two pairs of polarizing sunglasses (ordinary sunglasses won't do) or use two polarizing filters from a camera shop.

Place a clear plastic object in strong light and look at the object through the polarising materials.

To see the hidden stress lines simply rotate one of the polarizing lenses or filters until stress patterns like the ones shown on these pages appear.

This is a photograph of the top of a toothbrush holder in polarized light (see also page 30).

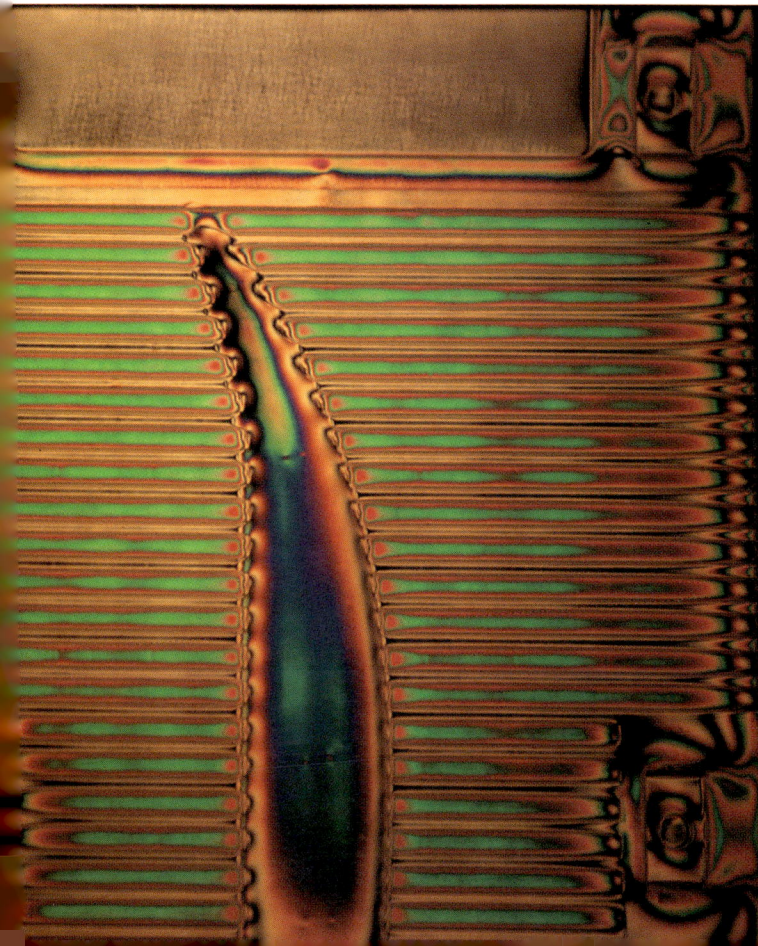

19

Changes with temperature

Every material will change size with temperature in its own special way. Some of them get dramatically bigger when they are warmed and shrink quickly when they are cooled. Others will show little change. This allows materials to be used in many different ways.

1 Bimetallic strip. Contacts apart, no electricity flows.

⚠️ **Take care with hot objects. Do not get unsealed electrical equipment near water.**

Using expansion and contraction

The regular expansion of liquids is used to make thermometers.

As the temperature rises or falls the liquid is forced to expand or contract in a very narrow tube. This amplifies the expansion and makes the changes easier to see.

2 Bimetallic strip has heated and made contact so that electricity flows.

Electric current flows to the heating element.

Heating element (in a fish tank the whole heater and switch would be safely enclosed in a sealed glass tube).

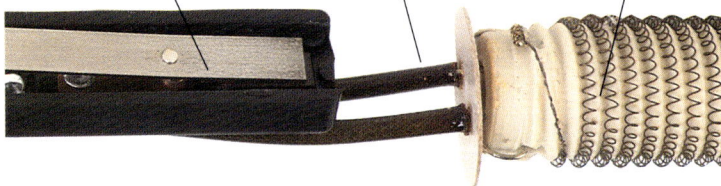

Switches can be designed to be activated by changes in temperature. One of the switch contacts is made of a strip of two different metals fixed firmly together. Each metal responds to a change of temperature differently, causing the strip to curl. The curling action can be used to complete a circuit or to break it.

Temperature-sensitive switches are used, for example, in home central heating systems and in tanks with tropical fish.

Alcohol inside a thermometer expands with temperature.

Heat conduction (relative):	
Copper	8000
Aluminium	4000
Brass	2500
Steel	1100
Pyrex glass	24
Concrete	2
Solid plastic	6
Rubber	2
Foamed plastic	1

Good conductors and poor conductors

Each material conducts heat in its own special way. A material that readily conducts heat is called a good conductor (and would be used in a heating radiator, for example), whereas a poor conductor would be used to insulate a house from extremes of weather.

This table give some values of how well heat is conducted. The larger the number the better it conducts heat. The aim is to find materials suitable to make an inexpensive radiator and a keep-cool food box. Which two materials would you use?

Straw

Cork or rubber bung

Water

Thermometer

Find out about the strange changes of water

You can measure the way water expands and contracts by using a plastic bottle and a straw. Make a small hole in the bottle cap just big enough to take the straw. Fit the straw and seal it to the cap with glue.

Put a thermometer in the bottle. Fill the bottle completely with water and fit the cap tightly so that it forces water up the straw. Mark the level and read off the temperature of the water from the thermometer.

Stand the bottle in a bucket and add warm water. Watch the liquid expand inside the straw, mark the new stable level and read the temperature. Next use ice water and watch the liquid shrink. Watch the level *very* carefully.

Many materials, such as this table spread, are designed to be plastic (easy to spread) at about 20 ^{0}C (room temperature). But what happens when they are warmed or cooled?

21

Electrical conduction

Materials that conduct electricity well are called conductors and those that conduct electricity poorly are called insulators. All electrical equipment uses materials with each of these properties.

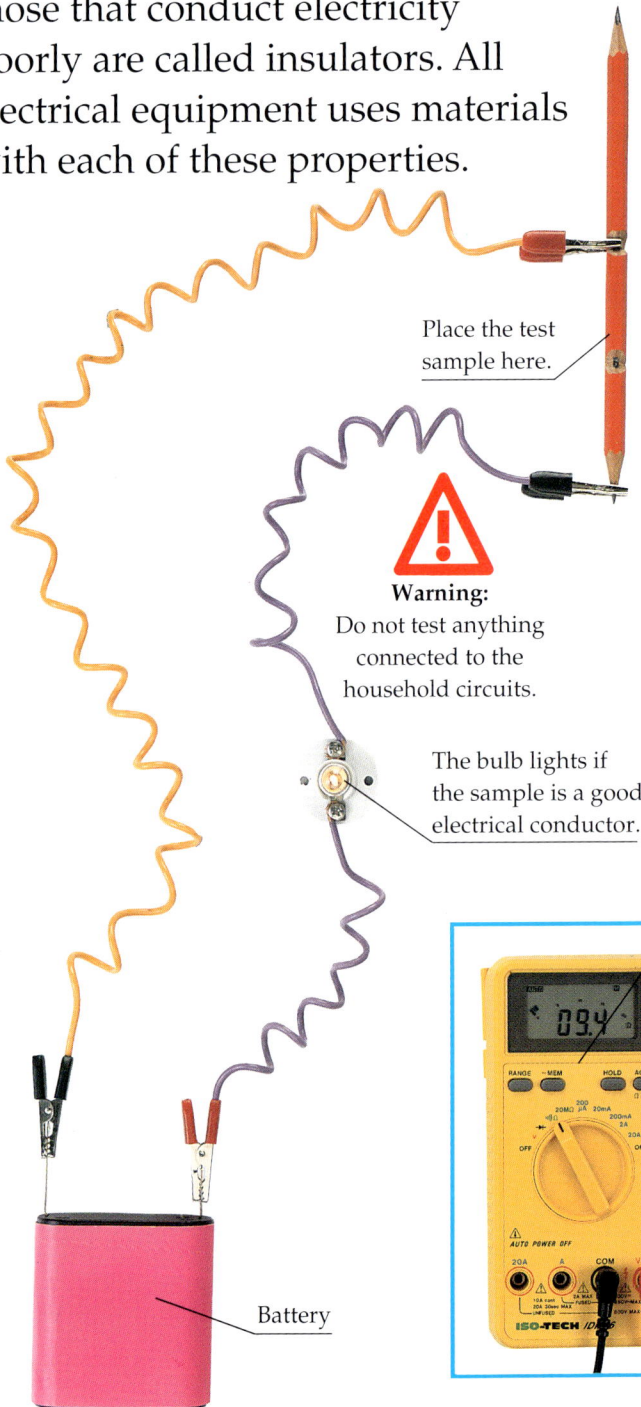

Place the test sample here.

Warning:
Do not test anything connected to the household circuits.

The bulb lights if the sample is a good electrical conductor.

Battery

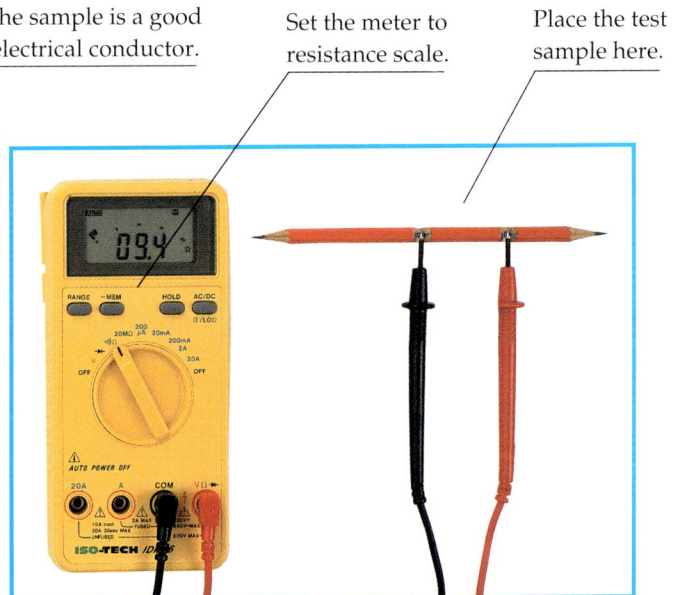

Set the meter to resistance scale.

Place the test sample here.

These are the kind of resistors found in most electronics equipment.

These resistors have been prepared on a strip for feeding to a robot circuit-board assembler.

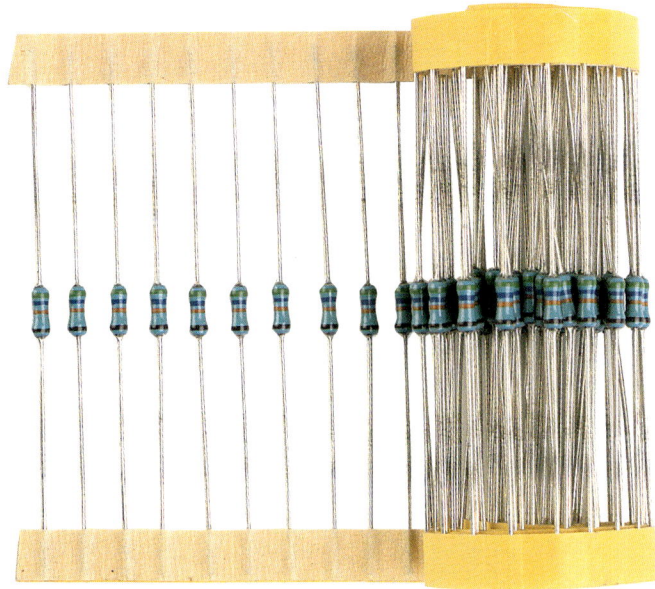

Each of the small electrical components shown above and to the right is a resistor. Each resistor is made of carbon powder enclosed in a plastic case. The wires are buried in the carbon to provide connections to electronic circuits.

Each resistor can be made to precise values. The coloured bands are codes that tell engineers the value of the resistance. For example the colour red is used for 2, orange for 3 and purple for 4.

Many uses for conduction

An electronic circuit relies on using the conducting properties of materials in many ways. Combinations of these components are found in computers, TVs and all circuits that use electrical signals.

The baseboard is made from plastic which is a good insulator.

The connections on this printed circuit board are made from copper because it is a good conductor.

A transistor is called a semi-conductor. By conducting electricity in a special way it can make electrical signals bigger.

Carbon resistors with colour-coded bands

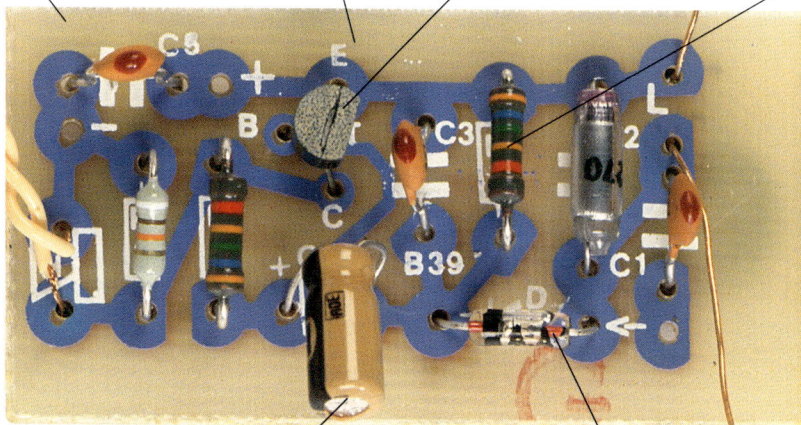

Capacitors are strips of conducting foil separated by strips of insulating plastic. They are used to store an electric charge.

(For more information on circuits and testing, see the books Electricity and Magnetism *and* Measuring *in the Science in our world series.)*

A diode is a component made of a material that has a large resistance if a current flows in one direction, but almost no resistance if the current flows in the opposite direction.

Hardness

Every type of material is made up in a particular way which gives it its own special characteristics. Hard materials are made of molecules very tightly held together, whereas soft materials have molecules that are easily pulled apart, sometimes one by one, sometimes in flakes.

When different materials are used together care is therefore needed to guard against unwanted scratching, rubbing and wearing.

Since earliest times, people have used hard stone for cutting. To find which ones were best they tested one stone on another. This is a stone made from volcanic lava that was fashioned into a hand tool some 5000 years ago.

Copper coin used for scratching surface to test hardness.

A selection of materials that can be tested for hardness.

How to test for hardness
The **hardness** of materials can be compared by using a simple test. You will need a copper coin, a knife and your thumbnail.

Make your test on some scrap material or on a corner that will not show. Start by scratching the material with a thumbnail. If it will not scratch, try the copper coin next and if that will not scratch, then try the knife.

Use the test to put these four items in order of hardness: a glazed wall tile, a piece of plastic, a piece of wood and a piece of paper.

Appropriate hardness

Pencils are made with leads having a wide range of hardness. Find pencils labelled 4B, 2B, HB, 2H and 4H. Each pencil is made for its own type of art work.

Write with each one in turn on a piece of normal writing paper. What is the difference between the effect of the 4B and the 4H?

By comparing all the pencils, can you decide why most people use an HB pencil when writing on ordinary grade paper?

See how materials change in hardness

Take a piece of frozen food from a freezer and try to cut it with an ordinary table knife. Frozen food has about the same hardness as a table knife which is why ordinary knives wont cut frozen food.

Now let the food thaw and try again – it should now cut easily. Finally cook the food and cut it once more. Cooking alters the fibres in the food, making the properties change.

A cake cutter doesn't have to have a particularly sharp edge because the difference in harness between the cutter and the cake mix is so great.

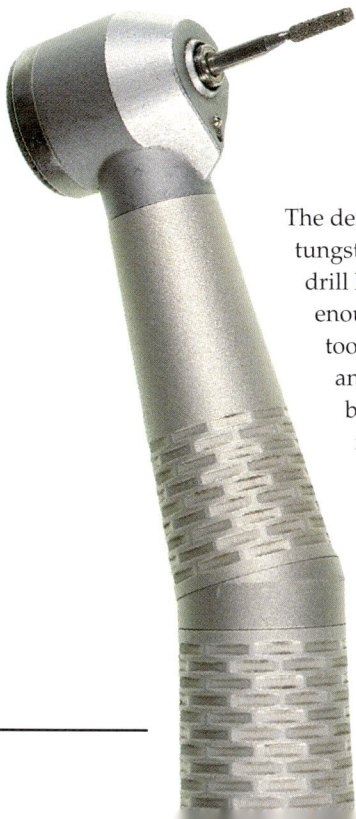

The dentist's diamond or tungsten carbide-tipped drill has to be hard enough to wear way tooth enamel quickly and not to become blunt. This is the reason there must be a large difference in hardness between cutter and tooth material.

Scissors have to be made of a very hard steel because otherwise they would quickly become blunt even when used to cut soft materials.

25

States of matter

Matter is found in three states – solid materials (for example ice), liquids (for example water), and gases (for example water vapour). Thus, if you heat a metal such as gold it will first become liquid and, if you heat it enough, it will disappear as it becomes a vapour.

Investigate changes in water
Water is one of the few common substance that occurs naturally on Earth in the three states: solid, liquid and gas.

Make a states of matter bowl by part filling a bowl with water. Place another bowl inside so that it floats and then put everything into the freezer.

When it is frozen take the glass bowls away and you will have a solid ice bowl. As it melts the solid becomes liquid and as the liquid evaporates the liquid turns to vapour.

Meteorologists use a thermometer wrapped in wet material (known as a wet bulb thermometer) to find out about the moisture, or humidity, in the air. By comparing the temperatures of a wet bulb and normal thermometer, the humidity can be calculated. As a general rule, the bigger the difference in temperature, the drier the air. When no more moisture can evaporate both thermometers read the same temperature.

Evaporation
Wrap a thermometer in a wet handkerchief and watch what happens to the temperature. The temperature should go down because heat energy is taken from the thermometer bulb and given to the water as it evaporates.

(For more information of the use of thermometers see the books Weather *and* Water *in the Science in our world series.)*

Energy for changing state

Energy is needed to change a solid into a liquid, as you know each time you heat some solid fat in a pan.

Energy is also needed to turn a liquid into a gas, which is why you have to boil water to make it turn quickly to steam.

From liquid to gas

Butane and propane are fuels that exist as gases at air pressure. A camping stove cylinder, however, is filled with butane or propane under enough pressure to make it turn liquid. This is done to increase the amount of fuel that can be contained in the cylinder.

When you turn the gas tap you open a valve and reduce the pressure, allowing some of the liquid to change into a gas.

When a liquid turns into a gas it draws heat energy from its surroundings, making the outside of the cylinder very cold indeed. This is why dew or frost sometime form on the cylinder even on a hot summer's day!

Liquid level inside the cylinder

This part of the cylinder goes very cold when the liquid changes state to become a gas.

27

Plastics (polymers)

The chemical name of many plastics commonly begins with the word poly. Poly means many, and plastics, properly known as **polymers**, are chemical compounds made in the form of linked chains containing many molecules.

Chemists have been able to make a wide variety of artificial polymers with specially designed properties, although, as you will see, no material is without its drawbacks.

Polymers dissolve in some types of cleaning fluids (known as solvents). This is the reason you are told to clean some polymers only with a clean damp cloth.

Polymers are very suitable for mass production of complicated parts because, while liquid they can be forced into a mould. They set very quickly and can then easily be removed from the mould.

Not only can some polymers burn easily but they can give off toxic fumes – polyurethane foams for example, release deadly hydrogen cyanide.

Polymers will not conduct electricity and so they can be used as insulating coatings for cables, for switch covers etc.

Look for signs of moulding
Polymers are forced into moulds through access tubes. Signs of the tube can be spotted on many products. Look for a slight bump with circular marks, like the one shown on the picture of the cog above.

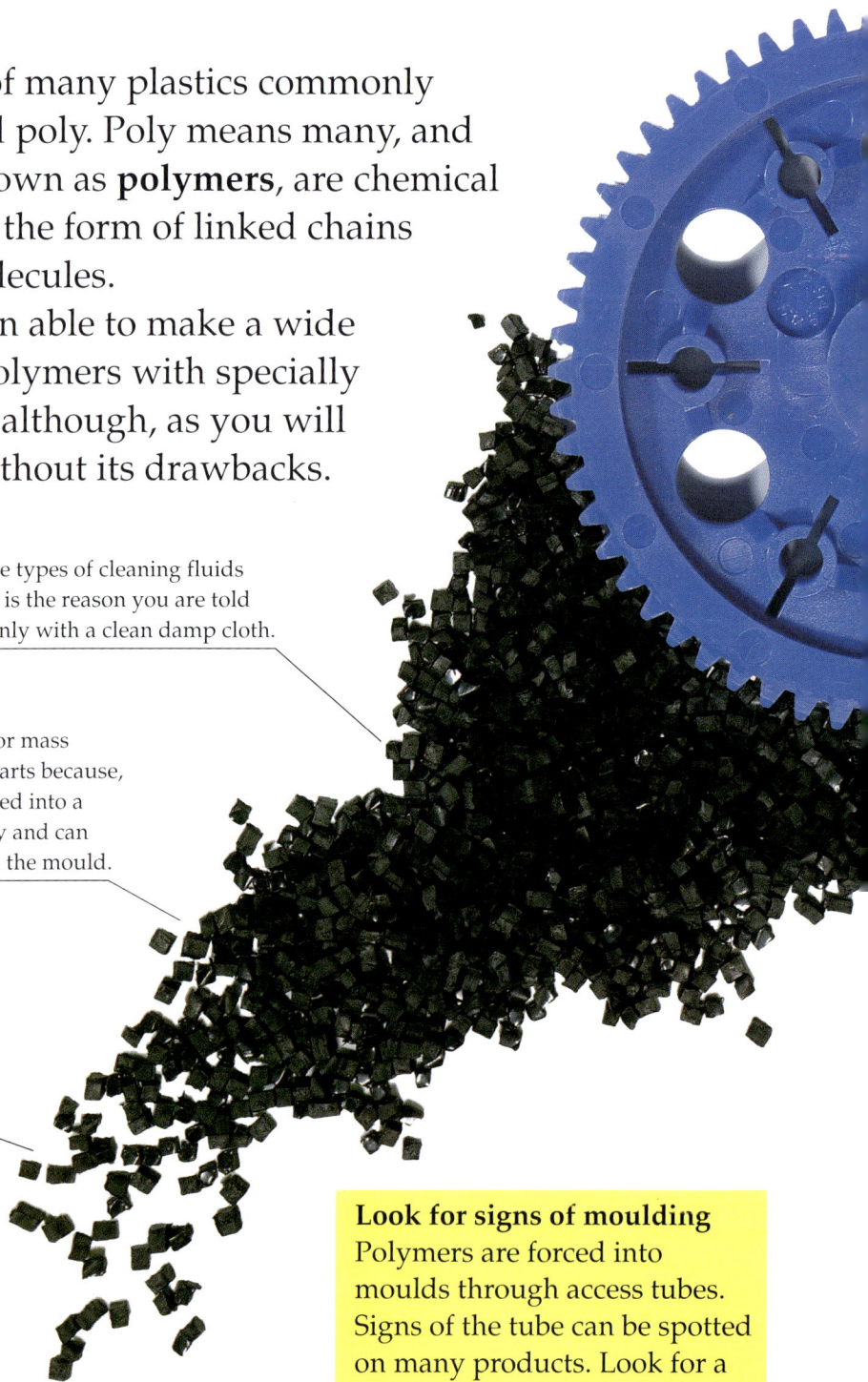

The elastic properties of polymers means they can be used as simple hinges such as snap-fasteners for sandwich bags.

Mould injection marks

Plastic bags are made of polythene which will not affect the taste of the food.

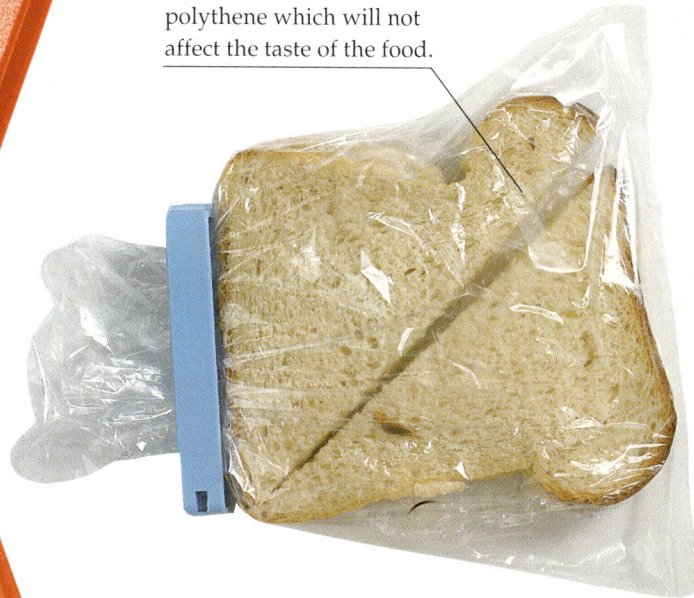

Polymers do not dissolve in water, nor do they let water through. For this reason they are used, for example, as bottles, and for water pipes.

This is an artificial lawn – sometimes used for sports grounds as it is easy to maintain.

CD cases are made of transparent plastic.

What kind of plastic is it?

Most plastics (polymers) can be made liquid for pouring or shaping, but they behave very differently after they have set.

There are two main kinds of plastic: thermoplastics, that go soft and melt when they are heated, and thermosets, that do not melt after they have set no matter how much they are heated.

Modern 'sealing wax' is often a thermoplastic.

A test for plastics
The only way to prove that a plastic is a thermoset or a thermoplastic is to heat it and find if it melts. As this is not a practical test, an almost foolproof, and easier, way is to know that most plastics are thermoplastics unless there is a good reason for them not to be. So ask: is this plastic likely to get really hot during use? If so, its a thermoset.

This toothbrush holder has been moulded using a thermoplastic. (See the enlargement on page 19.)

Shape a thermoplastic
Modern sealing wax is often made from a thermoplastic. Take a piece of sealing wax and light the wick. Melt a blob into a metal can lid and use a match stick or other former to mould it into shape before it sets. Then use a lighted match to melt the bob and mould it again, and again and again.

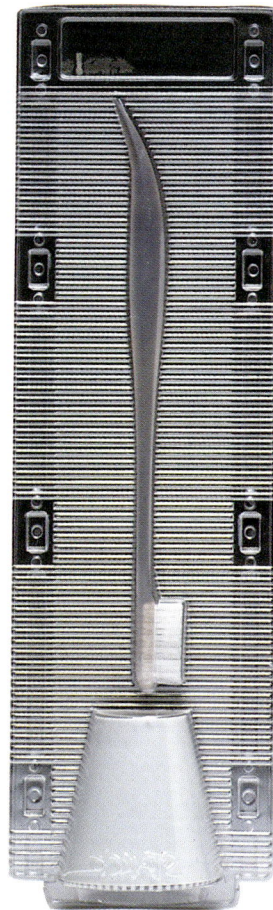

The chip on this circuit board may get hot and both the chip and the board must therefore be made of a thermoset.

Thermosets

These types of plastic are found in places where a hard, rigid, heat-resistant material is needed, such as for the handle (or all) of a spoon used in cooking, the circuit board for electronics and the plastic surfaces of kitchen units. Thermosets are usually brittle and more difficult to make than thermoplastics, so they are not used unless absolutely necessary.

The part of the case that hold the hotplate is a thermoset.

The handle and other parts of the iron do not get hot and they are made from thermoplastic.

The hot plate of the iron is made with metal coated in non-stick ceramic.

Metals

The casing for this piece of an automobile (a clutch plate) has been pressed into shape.

Metals are used to make many of our most important manufactured items where strength is required. Iron and steel are the most important metals. They are called the ferrous metals. Other important metals include aluminium, copper, zinc, nickel, tin, silver, and gold. These are all called nonferrous metals.

Using techniques such as drawing, rolling, pressing and casting they can be made into almost any shape.

PRESSED SHAPES

Pressed shapes
Metals often have plastic properties and they can be pressed into new shapes when hot or cold. Many of the panels of automobiles are pressed into shape, with the added bonus of greater strength as well as fine design.

Reflectors for lights are pressed out of thin metal into carefully controlled shapes. Then they are polished or coated in a reflective material until they act as mirrors.

This ship is made with large numbers of rolled steel plates.

FORGED AND ROLLED SHAPES

Forged and rolled shapes
Weight for weight metals are the strongest materials. They can also be rolled into sheets or hammered (forged) into many shapes. Steel is used where strength is needed, for example, in making ships and oil storage tanks.

TUBULAR SHAPES

Tubular shapes

One way to get strength without weight is to form metal into a tube. To make large diameter tubes sheet steel is folded over a rod and the join welded. By contrast, Small diameter tubes are extruded, a process similar to squeezing toothpaste from a tube.

The Forth Rail Bridge, Scotland, a masterpiece of tubular 'scaffolding'.

CAST SHAPES

This tap has been cast in brass and then plated with nickel and chromium for corrosion resistance and good looks.

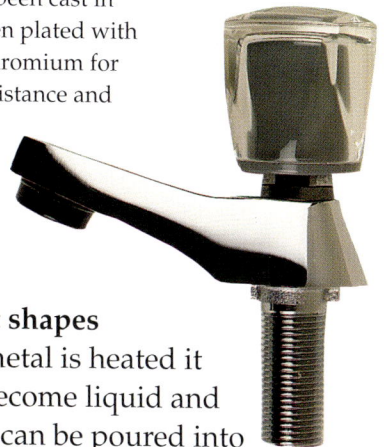

Cast shapes

If a metal is heated it will become liquid and then it can be poured into a mould to make a casting. Many taps are made of cast metal because taps receive a lot of heavy wear.

This classic steam train design has been cast in iron so that it can be used as a decorative door stop.

Working with metals

The science of metals is called metallurgy. By finding out about the properties of metals, and by combining them into new alloys, scientists have made metals some of the world's most useful materials.

Today even apparently simple mechanisms use a number of metals in order to keep down weight, increases strength, resist corrosion and save cost. Here are some examples.

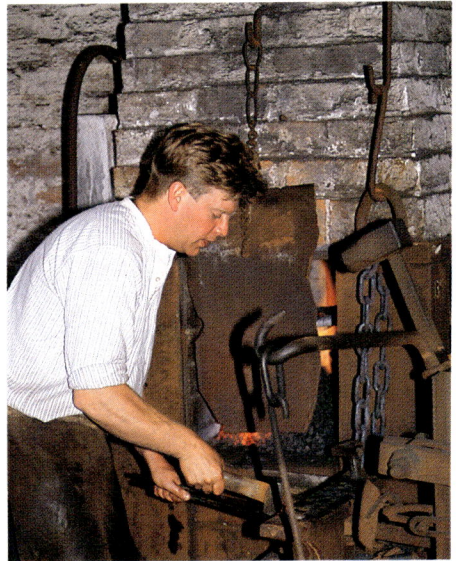
Hand-working steel to forge chain links.

A modern suspension bridge.

Matching metals and designs

Metals can be designed for many uses, and designs can be altered to suit the properties of the metal. Each bridge design, for example, takes the properties of the metal into account. The supporting cables will be made from a steel with a high resistance to breaking under tension (called tensile strength); while the bridge deck will be made of less specialised (and therefore less expensive) steel girders and plates.

Metals suited to craftwork

Copper was possibly the first metal used by people because it is soft, easily worked by hand, and it can be soldered. 'Raw', or native copper pieces can be beaten into shape, a technique called cold forging.

Molten copper was mixed to form alloys by a process of trial and error. Bronze (copper and zinc) was one of the first alloys. This alloy is easy to cast.

A bronze sculpture

Metals to make a door-lock

A door lock may seem a perfectly ordinary item of door furniture, but to stand up against intruders and the weather it has to be made of many metals, each of which is designed to use its properties to best advantage.

Carbon steel dead bolt. This must stand up to being forced by an intruder. This kind of steel cannot be cut easily.

Casing of stainless steel. The special steel is not needed for protection, but it is used to match the style of the outside covering.

Chromium plated knob for decorative purposes on the inside of the door.

Steel alloy where a decorative finish is not needed. This metal resists rusting but is cheaper than stainless steel and easier to bend into shape.

Strip of spring steel as part of locking mechanism.

Stainless steel cover. This steel is needed to protect the outside of the lock from harsh weather.

Chromium-plated brass key. The brass is easy to cut into shape and the chrome is used for decorative effect. The key does not have to be especially tough.

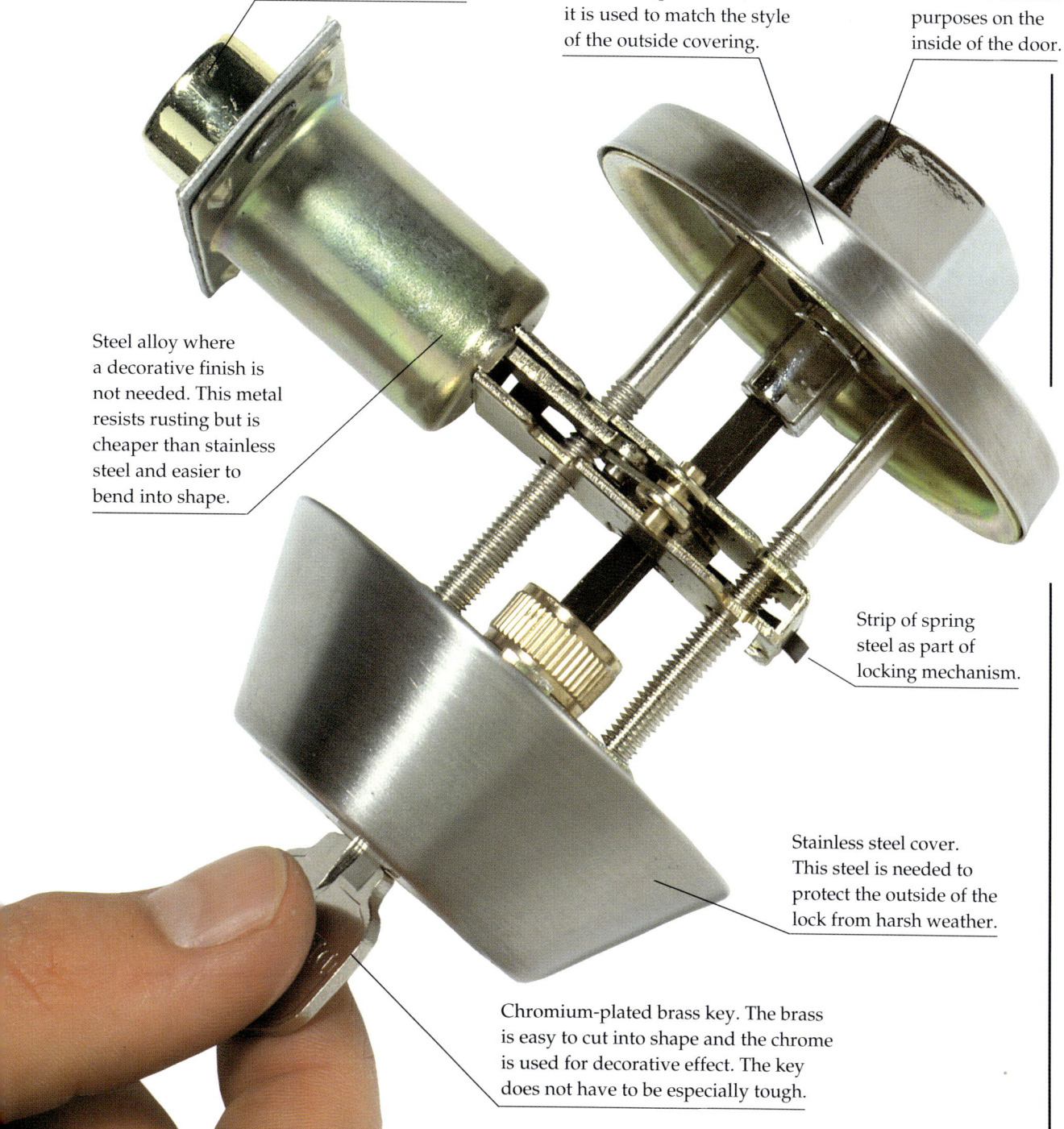

35

Corrosion and tarnishing

If you leave a metal object out in damp conditions it may change colour, and the surface may eventually become pitted or flaky. This is called corrosion. Rust, which affects iron and steel, is the most common type of corrosion. By treating metals with special chemicals, many forms of corrosion can be prevented.

Using one metal to protect another
Common metals corrode when in combination with others and water. For example, copper connected to zinc causes the zinc to corrode, and copper connected to iron causes the iron to corrode. This happens because water and two metals often act as a natural form of battery.

To protect the hulls of steel ships and the frames of oil rigs which are always in water, zinc blocks are placed on the steel below the water line. When the zinc blocks have corroded away they can easily be replaced with new blocks.

The Eiffel Tower, Paris has a workforce forever repainting the steel girders to prevent corrosion. It takes them so long to complete the job that when they get to the top it is time to start again at the bottom!

Protective chemicals
Salt water or rainwater with pollution gases dissolved in it (such as carbon dioxide and sulphur dioxide) make the 'battery effect' much more powerful, which is why unprotected cars corrode more rapidly in rainy cities or within reach of the spray from the sea.

Paint is a traditional chemical used to resist corrosion. Modern chemicals can now be made that react with the metal to make a corrosion-proof surface.

The process of tarnishing can be seen on copper coins. Look at the dates.

A rusted bolt

Nails corroding

Find the conditions for rust
You will need three jars with tops and about 12 bright shiny steel nails.

Put four of the nails in a jar and gently warm the jar in an oven or an airing cupboard. This will make sure that there is no moisture on the nails or the jar. Now close the jar tightly with its lid.

Boil some distilled water and put four more nails in another jar and fill the jar to the brim with the water.

Finally, put the last four nails in a jar with a few drops of tap water to make the inside damp.

Put the jars together on a windowsill and over the next few days watch what happens. Find out if rusting only happen when both air and water are present.

Tarnishing prevents good electrical contact. Gold and platinum are used to plate electrical contacts because they do not tarnish.

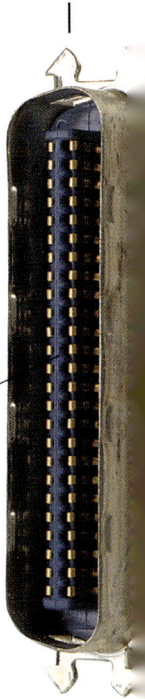

This is polythene-coated aluminium. The polythene prevents the fluids in the food from corroding the metal.

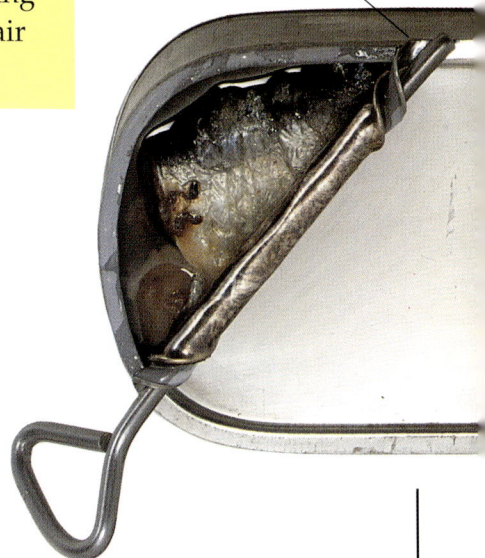

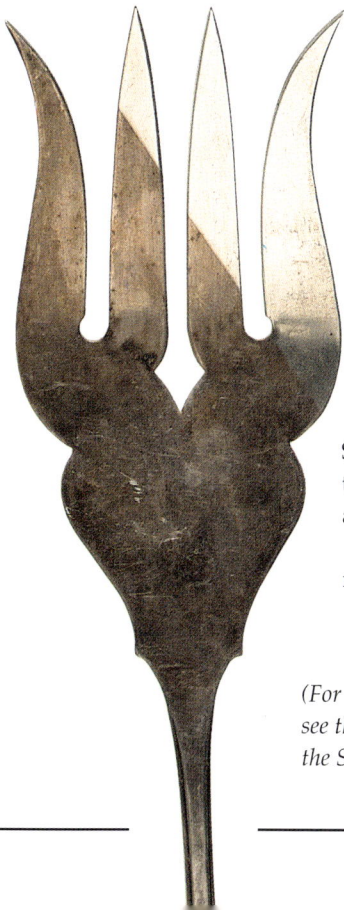

Some metals become dull when exposed to the air. Silver is a common example, as shown by the spoon on the left.

The dull, or **tarnished**, surface needs regular polishing to keep it bright.

(For more information on how batteries work see the book Electricity and Magnetism *in the Science in our world series.)*

Ceramics

Ceramic is the name given to materials produced by the heating of minerals such as sand and clay.

Some of the most common products made with ceramics are cement, concrete and glass, but others are now vital to the computer industry and include the silicon used to make computer chips. Even the fuel rods in nuclear reactors may be ceramics.

Work with clay

Many of the principles of the properties of ceramics can be seen by working with pottery clay. Following the steps on this page for making a piece of pottery will provide you with an interesting article and also show many of the properties of a ceramic.

Clay can be air dried or oven dried to speed the process.

1 Work (knead) the clay and then roll it into a sheet. Notice that the sheet is easy to bend and will probably not stand up on its own.
Cut the sheet into four and make an identical article with each piece.

2 Put one of the articles into an ordinary oven to dry out, then leave it to cool. Notice how the oven-dried clay is hard and brittle. If you soak it in water it will go soft again.

The effects of heat

Heating for a just few hours at about 100 – 200 ^{0}C boils away the water slowly and steadily. This is called drying.

If an article is heated – fired – at a high temperature (800 – 2000 ^{0}C) the ceramic material become fused into a rigid, strong, dense and non-porous object.

It is possible to produce a wide range of ceramics by varying the firing temperature, length of firing and the nature of the raw materials. It is even possible to get ceramics that are harder than metals. However, nearly all ceramics remain brittle.

Unglazed wall tile

Glazed kitchen tile

Kiln fired piggy-bank

Common ceramics

Traditional white-wares (bathroom bowls etc.) and porcelains contain a mineral called feldspar. This melts on firing at high temperatures (1400 ^{0}C) and coats (glazes) the clay and sand crystals. It not only holds the clay and sand together, but it makes the material watertight and gives a smooth, glassy, polished sheen.

Firing at about 1100 ^{0}C produces stoneware, a much rougher, but still waterproof ceramic. Below 1000 ^{0}C less melting occurs and the pores in the ceramic are not sealed up. This rough material is called earthenware.

3 If your school has a pottery kiln, put one piece of the clay sheet into the kiln and fire it, then leave it to cool. The kiln fired clay will be like a piece of pottery. It will not go soft when wetted, showing that it has been changed into new minerals with new properties.

4 The final article can be glaze-brushed with a mixture of powdered glass and colouring materials – and then fired again. This will give it a smooth, glassy and waterproof coating.

Glazed clay

Glass

Common glass is made by heating a mixture of sand, soda and limestone to about 1300 ^{0}C. The mixture is then cooled in such a way that crystals do not develop. There are many types of glass, each dependent on the raw materials originally used.

Moulded glass

Glass containers such as bottles, vases, light bulbs and jars are made by blowing hot blobs or ribbons of glass into moulds on a continuous machine.

Soda-lime glass

Over 90 per cent of glass made today is called soda-lime glass because soda is the main raw material along with sand and limestone. Soda-lime glass can be melted at a relatively low temperature and it is cheap to make. Unfortunately it also expands and contracts greatly with temperature and so cannot be used to make cookware. Its main use is for windows and bottles.

Tempering

Glass can be strengthened by cooling the surface quickly. This is called tempering.

Tempering causes the surface to become solid, and as the inside solidifies and contracts, it pulls on the surface, putting it under continual stress. Tempered glass – sometimes called toughened glass – is used as safety glass for automobile side windows and patio doors.

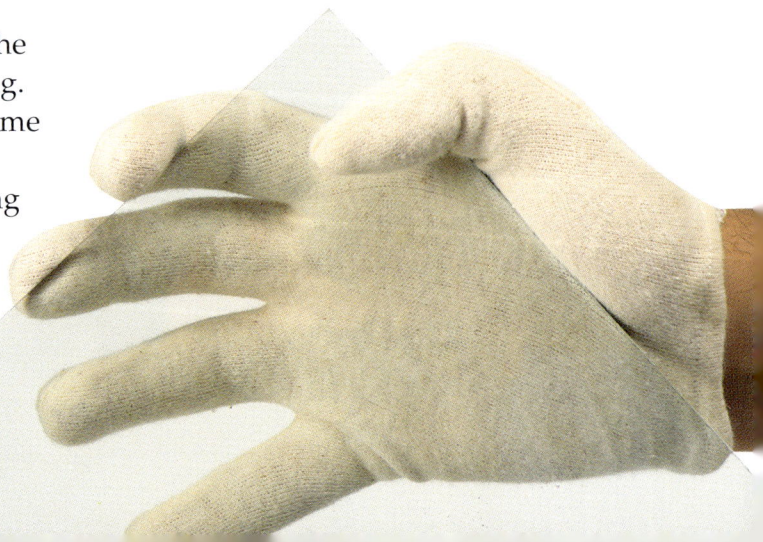

Coloured glass

Glass can be coloured by adding, for example, copper (for red and blue colours); iron or chromium (for green) and iron and sulphur (for brown).

A blue glass wine bottle used to denote the region in Germany from which the wine comes.

Most flat glass, such as that used to make the office windows shown in the picture above, is made continuously in large tanks through a process known as float glass making. It was invented by the English technologist Sir Alistair Pilkington.

The powdered raw materials are fed in at one end, and a molten strip or plate of glass emerges at the other.

Borosilicate glass

This is a type of glass which does not change size very much on heating and cooling and so it can be used in the cooker and the freezer.

It is made with boric oxide and very little soda. Many people know oven glass under the trade name Pyrex.

A cookware glass container

Which glass is it?
A sheet of tempered glass does not look any different from float glass, but it is much safer. If you look on the side windows of vehicles there will be a little mark etched on. This indicates the kind of glass it is and the standard to which it has been made.

Composites and laminates

Many materials are used in combination to give a new material that is better than either.

Composites are created by embedding one material inside the other to reinforce it. Vehicle tyres, for example, are rubber reinforced with steel wires.

Laminates are materials made of several layers glued together. Corrugated cardboard and plywood are common examples of a laminate.

This concrete building is being constructed with steel reinforcing rods in the columns and steel meshes in the floors and walls.

The metal wires set inside the rubber can be seen clearly on this tyre cross-section.

Experiment with composites

Collect some straw and cut it into small pieces. Notice that straw stems are like tubes. Mix the straw into wet pottery clay then roll it into a sheet. What properties does this composite have that are different from a clay sheet?

Fibre reinforced materials

When fibres are used in a composite the fibres (such as glass fibres in a resin) carry the load and stiffen the material. Ceramics are often used for the fibres even though the ceramic fibres are brittle. By embedding the strong fibres in a flexible matrix it is possible to get strength and flexibility.

Plywood is a common laminate made from sheets of wood glued together.

Adhesives

An adhesive is a substance that will join two materials together to make a laminate. Adhesives are often popularly called glues.

For an adhesive to work effectively it must flow over the surfaces to be joined. The adhesive flows into minute crevices on the material surface, and this is the reason surfaces are roughened before bonding.

This plain-looking coffee bag may consists of several quite different layers of material to make a laminate. One layer keeps out moisture, another stops the flavour escaping while yet others provide colour and strength.

Front windscreens are laminated, that is there are two sheets of glass sandwiching a plastic film. If the glass should fracture in an accident the plastic holds the broken fragments in place. Bullet proof glass is simply a multi-layered 'sandwich'.

Materials and the environment

In time natural processes will slowly recycle everything we use, building new rocks from old materials. However, in the short term there can be massive damage to the natural world as industrial processes create vast quarries, create huge spoil mounds and release liquids into the rivers and seas that may be deadly (toxic) to people, plants and animals.

This is why it is extremely important to think not just how useful materials might be, but also how their use affects the environment. Here are some examples of the problems caused, and how a little thought can help our planet's future.

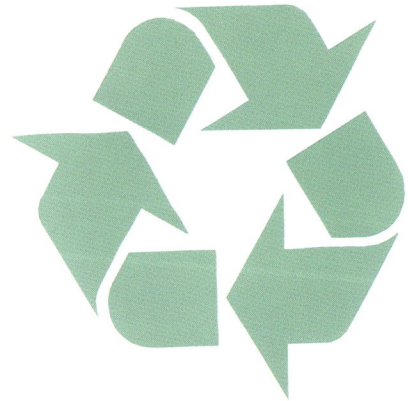

Better use of plastics
For decades people have been producing polymers (plastics) that will not rot away or safely burn and that cannot be used again. The only thing that can be done is to bury them. This is clearly an unacceptable solution for the future, which is the reason more and more products are being made of polymers that can be recycled.

Disposable materials
Various types of plastics are used for disposable cups. Can you think of the advantages of using the plastic cups shown here? What are the disadvantages in terms of litter control? What other material might be more suitable?

Plastic cup

Lead ore

Spoil from mining

Mining is an extremely important activity because it provides us with the raw materials we need. But mining also needs great care because it creates vast – and often unsightly – holes in the ground and also very large quantities of unwanted rock waste called spoil. The signs of toxic spoil tips and waste water are easy to see because nothing will grow where the ground is polluted.

The picture on the right shows a town that has been ruined by careless mining during a rush to supply minerals for industry. Enormous scientific effort is now having to be applied to discover ways of neutralising the toxic waste. This problem might have been lessened if there had been a better understanding of the long-term effects.

Reusing materials

As it becomes possible to recycle more and more materials, there is less need to quarry and mine the Earth to find new resources.

Recycling, rather than burying wastes in landfill sites such as old quarries, is also one way of saving energy.

(For more information about environmental matters see the books Don't throw it away *and* Don't waste energy *in the Science in our world series.)*

45

New words

adhesive
a material, often known as 'glue' which can be used to join other materials

brittle
the state of a material such that it is liable to break (fracture) when stressed

cell
the simplest living part of life. A cell contains all the information needed to make new cells. Human bodies contain thousands of millions of cell

conduct
the way some materials can transfer electricity or heat. Materials which do not easily act as conductors are called insulators

corrode
the process where the elements of the weather or water begin to act chemically on a metal or other material so that its surface becomes pitted and it loses its strength

deform
to change shape. Materials may deform permanently or they may go back to their original shape if the force is removed or sometimes if they are heated

elastic
the way a material will return to its original shape after it has been stretched, squashed or deformed in some other way. Rubber is a good example of an elastic material

element
a substance that cannot be broken down into simpler substances by chemical means

fibre
Plant tissues are made of a material called cellulose. The bark and trunks of trees are hard forms of cellulose which, when treated with chemicals, separate out into fibres

hardness
the way materials can stand up to wear, scratching or being marked. Materials can be grouped into various degrees of hardness. A scratching tool, for example, a glass cutter, has to be very hard, and the best ones have diamond tips, although special steels can also be used

industrial revolution
the time, beginning in Britain in the eighteenth century and lasting through the nineteenth century, when the factory system was developed

inorganic material
any material that does not contain the element carbon

manufacture
the industrial processing of materials to make them into new shapes

mass-produced
the manufacture of many standard items on a factory production line

mineral
people in industry think of a mineral as a substance that can be dug from the ground and which can be used to make things when it has been properly processed. Clay, limestone and sand are common examples

organic material
any material that contains the element carbon

plastic (to stretch)
the way material will change shape and remain in that new shape when it is squeezed, stretched or deformed.
    Steel is plastic because it can be made into new shapes such as cans

plastic (material)
these are materials – really called polymers – made mostly from oil and wood-based chemicals. Some can be pushed into a new shape (they are plastic), whereas others break when a force is used (they are brittle). Unfortunately the commonly used word plastic describing material can be confused with the technical word meaning to change shape, which is the reason people have to be careful how they use the word plastic

polymer
any substance that formed from long linked chains of molecules

pulp
the mashed up mix of wood fibres and water that is produced during paper-making

raw material
a material that is used as the basis of some form of processing

refine
to make more pure. A chemical refinery takes a mixture of substances, such as are found in crude oil, and separates out the useful constituents. Metals are refined by taking away impurities. A blast furnace helps to refine iron ore

strength
of a material is a way of describing how well a material will stand up to a stretching, twisting, bending or squashing force without breaking

stress and strain
a stress is the force, such as pulling or pushing, applied over the area of an object. When the material changes shape because of the force, the movement is called a strain

synthetic material
any material that is made by people in a factory or workshop and which would not occur naturally. The largest groups of synthetic materials are the polymers (plastics)

Index